	DATE DUE		
OC 28 '02			

COSTUME, TRADITION, AND CULTURE:
REFLECTING ON THE PAST

Wonders of the Ancient World

by

Therese De Angelis

Chelsea House Publishers
Philadelphia

CHELSEA HOUSE PUBLISHERS

Editor-in-Chief Stephen Reginald
Managing Editor James D. Gallagher
Production Manager Pamela Loos
Art Director Sara Davis
Picture Editor Judy Hasday
Senior Production Editor Lisa Chippendale
Designers Takeshi Takahashi

3 5 7 9 8 6 4 2

Library of Congress Cataloging-in-Publication Data

De Angelis, Therese.
Wonders of the ancient world / by Therese De Angelis.

  p. cm. — (Costume, tradition, and culture: reflecting on the past)
Includes bibliographical references and index.
Summary: In text and photographs, describes twenty–five ancient architectural wonders, including the Great Wall of China, the Kukulcan Pyramid in Mexico, and the Avenue of the Lions in Greece.

ISBN 0–7910–5170–6 (hardcover)
1. History, Ancient—Miscellanea—Juvenile literature.
2. Curiosities and wonders—Juvenile literature. 3. Building, Stone—Juvenile literature. [1. History, Ancient—Miscellanea. 2. Curiosities and wonders. 3. Architecture.] I. Title. II. Series.
D62.D39   1998   98–35808
930—dc21   CIP
                                   AC

CONTENTS

INTRODUCTION

For as long as people have known that other cultures existed, they have been curious about the differences in their customs and traditions. Julius Caesar, the famous Roman leader, wrote long chronicles about the inhabitants of Gaul (modern-day France) while he was leading troops in the Gallic Wars (58–51 B.C.). In the chronicles, he discussed their religious beliefs, their customs, their day-to-day life, and the conflicts among the different groups. Explorers like Marco Polo traveled thousands of miles and devoted years of their lives to learning about the peoples of the East and bringing home the stories of Chinese court life, along with the silks, spices, and inventions of that culture. The Chelsea House series *Costume, Tradition, and Culture: Reflecting on the Past* continues this legacy of exploration and discovery by discussing some of the most fascinating traditions, beliefs, legends, and artifacts from around the world.

Different cultures develop traditions and costumes to mark the roles of people in their societies, to commemorate events in their histories, and to make the changes and mysteries of life more meaningful. Soldiers wear uniforms to show that they are serving in their nation's army, and insignia on the uniforms show what ranks they hold within the army. People of Bukhara, a city in Uzbekistan, have for centuries woven fine threads of gold into their clothes, and when they travel to other cities they can be recognized as Bukharans by the golden embroidery on their traditional costume. For many years, in the Irish countryside, people would leave bowls of milk outside at night as an offering to the fairies, or "Good People," believing that this would help ensure their favor and keep the family safe from fairy mischief. In Mexico, November 2 is the Day of the Dead, when people visit cemeteries and have feasts to remember their ancestors. In the United States, brides wear white dresses, and the traditional wedding includes many rituals: the father of the bride "giving her away" to the groom, the exchange of vows and rings, the throwing of rice, the tossing of the bride's bouquet. These rituals and symbols help make the marriage meaningful and special for the couple, their families, and their friends, by expressing the change that is taking place and allowing the friends and families to wish luck to the couple.

This series will explore some of the myths, symbols, costumes, and traditions of various cultures from around the world and different times in the past. *Fighting Units of the American War of Independence,* for example, will detail the uniforms, weapons, and decorations of the regiments and battalions on both sides of the war, along with the battles in which they became famous. *Roman Myths, Heroes, and Legends* describes how the ancient Romans explained the wonders and natural phenomena of their world with fantastic stories of superhuman heroes and almost human deities who could change the course of history at will. In *Popular Superstitions,* you will learn how some familiar superstitious beliefs—such as throwing spilled salt over your shoulder, or hanging a horseshoe over your door for good luck—originally began, in times when people feared that devils and evil spirits were meddling in their lives. Few people still believe in malicious spirits, but many still toss the spilled salt over their shoulders, or knock on wood when expressing cautious hope. The legendary figures of a culture—the brave explorers of *The Wild West* or the wicked brigands described in *Infamous Pirates*—help shape that culture's values by providing grand, almost mythical examples of what people should (or should not!) strive to be.

The illustrations that accompany these books have their own cultural history. Originally, they were printed on small collectors' cards and sold in the early 20th century. Each card in a set of 25 or 50 would depict a different person, artifact, or event, and usually the reverse side would offer a few sentences of description to explain the picture. Now, they provide a fascinating glimpse into history and an entertaining addition to the stories presented here.

ABOUT THE AUTHOR

THERESE DE ANGELIS holds an M.A. in English Literature from Villanova University and studied rare book cataloging and preservation at Columbia University. She was the contributing editor for a number of Chelsea House titles, including *The Black Muslims, Rosie O'Donnell,* and *Jewish Women Fiction Writers.* She is also the author of *Native Americans* and *The Spanish* in Chelsea House's Indians of North America series, and *Louis Farrakhan* in the Black Americans of Achievement series.

OVERVIEW

Wonders of the Ancient World

Relics of previous cultures—cooking and hunting instruments; drawings and writings on stone, animal skin, or cloth; weapons and farming tools—all provide a glimpse into the daily lives and customs of civilizations past. Yet perhaps no other remnants of bygone cultures are as fascinating as the marvels of ancient architecture that have withstood hundreds or thousands of years of harsh weather and changing fortunes.

The science of archaeology is only about 200 years old, though its origins date to the 15th century, when Renaissance Europeans began seeking information about the empires of ancient Greece and Rome. Not until the 18th century, when the ruins of the Roman cities of Pompeii and Herculaneum were discovered, did the process of excavation become exacting and methodical. Egyptian archaeology, for example, began in 1798, when the French emperor Napoleon Bonaparte invaded the country and brought scholars and historians to catalog its remains.

Nineteenth-century advances in geology and anthropology also helped advance archaeology. The idea that artifacts could be dated by their position in the strata (or layers) of the earth revolutionized the discipline, and Charles Darwin's theory of human evolution, which suggested that man had a much longer history than previously imagined, inspired an even broader interest in ancient cultures. The discovery of prehistoric Indus Valley and Chinese civilizations, as well as the Olmec culture of North America, were results of that enthusiasm.

By examining who built the temples, monuments, and cities of ancient cultures, how they did it, and why, we will gain a greater understanding of our own world.

COLOSSI OF
MEMNON

THEBES, EGYPT, 14TH CENTURY B.C.

Thousands of years ago, the city of Thebes, Egypt, flourished where the cities of Karnak and Luxor stand today. Among the many architectural remains of the magnificent ancient city are the Colossi of Memnon, a pair of monolithic statues representing the *ka* (soul) of Pharaoh Amenhotep III, who reigned from 1390 to 1352 B.C. The statues, each 60 feet high, originally stood in front of the mortuary temple of Amenhotep, which is now gone. The temple was the largest in Thebes, with an interior measuring 88 acres.

Over time, the temple's stones were removed by succeeding pharaohs for use in erecting their own memorials. The annual flooding of the Nile and the plowing of land also contributed to its disappearance. The symbolism of the colossi was also lost over the years, and the ancient Greeks eventually decided that they represented two fabled heroes

who fought in the Trojan War: Memnon, the son of Eos, the goddess of the dawn; and Tithonus.

In A.D. 27 an earthquake cracked one of the statues, and it became famous for its "singing" or whistling sounds at daybreak (it was believed that Memnon was greeting his mother, Eos, each morning). Evidence that ancient Greek and Roman tourists visited the site is seen in the graffiti covering its legs and torso. After the statue was repaired in the third century A.D., the singing ceased. Today, the Colossi of Memnon, the ancient guardians of Thebes, sit alone in an empty field, near a road leading from the Nile to the edge of the Sahara Desert.

EL JEM
COLOSSEUM

EL JEM, TUNISIA, THIRD CENTURY A.D.

n its last 1,000 years, the ancient Egyptian empire was invaded by a succession of foreigners—Sudanese, Persians, Macedonians, Greeks, and finally Romans, who took power in 30 B.C. The massive colosseum (amphitheater) at El Jem, much of which remains today, is viewed by many to be the grandest structure ever built by the Romans in Africa. At the time it was constructed, it was the sixth largest amphitheater in the Roman Empire, which extended into Europe, North Africa, and the Middle East. Today it is second in size only to the famous Colosseum in Rome.

The El Jem Colosseum is made of limestone and is elliptical in shape, measuring 485 feet across at its widest and rising to 120 feet. The galleries (what we call "stands" in modern arenas) are 60 feet wide; the interior measures up to 300 feet. The colosseum held more than 30,000 people—about

the same capacity as baseball's Fenway Park in Boston, Mass-
achusetts.

What did these ancient crowds come to see? The most
popular events were gladiator fights and staged wild animal
hunts. But there were other, more savage spectacles: bloodthirsty crowds not only watched fierce beasts tearing each
other to pieces but also observed the savage animals attack-
ing and killing humans. The elongated pit shown in this
photograph led to underground chambers, where human
and animal "prey" were imprisoned until they were brought
above ground for competitions. Today the El Jem Colosseum
sits in the midst of a flat plain in Tunisia, a relic of an ancient
and powerful empire.

GREAT PYRAMIDS

GIZA, EGYPT, C. 2600–2500 B.C.

"Time laughs at all things," an old Arab proverb goes, "but the pyramids laugh at time." The saying described the pyramid complex at Giza, the oldest of the Seven Wonders of the Ancient World and the only one remaining.

The largest and oldest of the Giza pyramids is the Great Pyramid of Khufu (or Cheops), who ruled Egypt c. 2600 B.C. It was originally 481 feet tall and measures 756 feet on each side of its base. An estimated 2.3 million stone blocks weighing 6.5 million tons went into its construction; the stones were so precisely laid that the blade of a knife will not fit between them. Inside the pyramid is a system of shafts, galleries, and hidden rooms, including the King's Chamber, believed to be the burial vault of Khufu.

The pyramid of King Khafre (or Chephren), Khufu's son, is 10 feet shorter and 48 feet narrower at its base than the Great Pyramid, although it looks larger because it sits on

a higher base. The smallest of the three main structures, the 218-foot Pyramid of Menkaure (or Mycerinus), was erected by Khafre's son.

The great pyramids were originally faced with smooth white limestone, which must have gleamed in the desert sun. Today, only a fragment of this facing remains as a cap on the Pyramid of Khafre. Legends of great treasures buried with the pharaohs have persisted over the ages. But though builders sealed internal passages with huge stone blocks, by 1000 B.C. every known pyramid had been looted. The Italian adventurer Giovanni Belzoni, the first European ever to enter the Great Pyramid, in 1818, found the main burial chamber empty of all but a granite sarcophagus.

GREAT SPHINX

GIZA, EGYPT, C. 2500 B.C.

The Great Sphinx at Giza is one of the most mysterious—and famous—structures in the world. For at least 4,500 years this huge sculpture with the head of a king and the body of a crouching lion has stared into the desert, a mute witness to centuries of Egyptian history.

No one knows exactly how old the Sphinx (Greek for "strangler") is, but most archaeologists date it from the time of the pharaoh Khafre, for whom one of the nearby pyramids was built around 2480 B.C. The sculpture, which measures 200 feet long and 65 feet high, was carved from an outcrop of limestone, a soft stone unsuitable for the huge building blocks used to build the pyramids.

Who does the Sphinx represent? Many historians believe it is Khafre himself. They point out that the head is dressed in the *nemes* headcloth, a symbol of royalty. At one time, the statue had a long, narrow, ritual beard, added probably 1,000

years after its completion. It is also missing its nose, as well as the *uraeus* (sacred cobra) from its headdress.

For most of its life the Sphinx was buried up to its neck in shifting desert sands. But in the 15th century B.C., a prince who was to become King Thutmose IV fell asleep under the Sphinx and was told in a dream to clear away the sand. In return the Sphinx promised to make him a king. Over time other attempts were made to clear the sand, and the Sphinx was finally dug out in 1925. But due to exposure the soft limestone has been badly eroded; it was probably safer from the elements when buried. A total restoration of the Sphinx was completed in the 1990s.

TEMPLE OF LUXOR

LUXOR, EGYPT, C. 1400–1300 B.C.

The ancient city of Thebes was once home to the godlike pharaohs who ruled Egypt during what is known as the 18th Dynasty (1610–715 B.C.). The pharaohs lived in unparalleled splendor in huge palaces, with storehouses full of riches gathered from conquered lands. They also built vast temples dedicated to patron gods; each ruler was entombed in one of his temples after death.

The most famous temples in Egypt are those of Luxor and Karnak, two cities that occupy the site of Thebes. The Temple of Luxor was begun during the reign of Amenhotep III (c. 1411–1375 B.C.), but several succeeding kings contributed to its construction.

The principal entrance to the complex today is an imposing gateway called the Pylon of Rameses II (shown here). In front of the pylon were two 46-foot statues of Rameses II and a pair of 80-foot obelisks covered with

hieroglyphs (a pictorial system of writing used by ancient Egyptians). One of these obelisks now stands in the Place de la Concorde in Paris, France.

Beyond the entrance is the immense Court of Rameses II, lined by colonnades and huge statues of the pharaoh. In the court's northeast corner is the tiny Mosque of Abu el-Haggag, built years later by Arab conquerors of Egypt. At one time, one of the temple chambers also was converted by early Christians into a church.

The Avenue of the Sphinxes, a two-mile path lined with human-headed animals, connected the Temple of Luxor with its counterpart at Karnak. Though smaller and less elaborate than Karnak, the Temple of Luxor is a superb example of the sculpture and architecture of ancient Egypt.

ANANDA TEMPLE

he ancient religious precinct of Pagan was once the capital of Burma (now Myanmar). In 1044, when King Anawrahta conquered the Mon civilization, he captured its royal family, scores of skilled artisans, and many Buddhist monks, forcing them to settle in Pagan. Aware of their sophisticated culture, Anawrahta set the captives to work organizing the newly united kingdom of Burma.

Today Pagan is home to the greatest surviving group of brick and plaster structures in South Asia, nearly all of them religious buildings. More than 2,000 temples and temple remains are scattered across an area of roughly 10 miles. Perhaps the most impressive of these structures is the Ananda Temple, which was dedicated in 1090.

Ananda is one of scores of buildings called *cetiyas* that combine the attributes of a stupa—a solid building that the faithful can walk around but cannot enter—and a shrine. The multiple terraces rising from the base of the building were a new design, meant to symbolize a sacred mountain.

Unlike a stupa, Ananda is open inside, with entrance vestibules projecting from all four sides. From its 30-foot-high two-tiered base, six terraces rise in a pyramid shape and meet in an ornate, elongated gold spire rising 168 feet above the ground. Both the base and the terraces were decorated in glazed plaques; in modern times the temple has been painted a brilliant white with lime stucco.

In the center of the shrine are four enormous standing Buddhas, each facing one of the four points of the compass. Unlike most of the temples in the region, this magnificent, thousand-year-old shrine is still in use today.

ANGKOR WAT

ANGKOR, CAMBODIA, C. A.D. 1113–1150

For five centuries beginning in the ninth century A.D., the powerful Khmer empire ruled over most of what is now called Indochina—Thailand, Cambodia, Laos, and southern Vietnam. The capital of the Khmer empire was Angkor, where in the 12th century King Suryavarman II ordered the construction of a vast temple called Angkor Wat.

Angkor Wat is situated on an island and surrounded by a wide moat. A single causeway (or bridge) spanning the moat allows the approaching guest to experience the full effect of the temple's architectural splendor. After passing through a great doorway, the visitor enters a huge gallery. A series of staircases and terraces leads from an outer courtyard to a central courtyard and finally to a huge central tower. Ornamental pools throughout the complex reflect the temple's many towers and add to its beauty.

Amazingly, the vast temple was constructed without mortar and has almost no foundations, yet it remains nearly intact 1,000 years later. Only iron bars driven into stones—and the temple's own weight—hold the masonry together. One striking feature of Angkor Wat is its many-tiered towers, star-shaped at their peaks.

The archaeologists who discovered Angkor Wat in 1861 were puzzled by the curious mix of Hindu and Buddhist decorations covering its walls. Later historians learned that the Khmer religion incorporated beliefs from both religions, and that the design of Angkor Wat was meant to imitate the five peaks of Mount Meru, the center of the universe for Hindus and Buddhists. The Khmer people also believed that their kings were gods; when King Suryavarman II died in 1150, the magnificent temple became his tomb.

BUDDHA OF KAMAKURA

KAMAKURA, JAPAN, A.D. 1252

he Great Buddha, or "Daibatsu," of Kamakura is one of many enormous Buddha images made to imitate the colossal statues of China. The first Daibatsu in Japan was the eighth-century bronze statue at the Todai-ji temple in Nara near Kyoto, which measures more than 53 feet high and weighs 452 tons.

Although smaller than the statue at Nara, the Daibatsu of Kamakura is the most famous of Japan's Great Buddha statues. Forged out of bronze in 1252 by the well-known sculptor Ono Goroemon, the statue measures 42 feet high and weighs 103 tons.

Its hollow interior contains a staircase leading to the figure's shoulders. Like the statue at Nara, the Diabatsu of Kamakura is portrayed in a seated position, palms facing upward and resting in its lap, on a pedestal shaped like an open lotus flower. It now sits outdoors but was originally sit-

uated in the center of a fine temple that was destroyed by storms, rebuilt, and then swept away by a tidal wave around 1495.

The Daibatsu of Kamakura represents Amida, the Buddha of Endless Light, who was popular in 13th-century Japan. A 30-pound silver ornament in the center of its forehead signifies the light emanating from the god itself.

GREAT STUPA

SANCHI, INDIA, C. 250 B.C.

Sanchi, India, is widely known for its numerous monasteries, temples, and stupas—huge burial mounds faced with brick or stone that hold holy relics of Buddha. One of the most famous Buddhist monuments is the Great Stupa at Sanchi. Made of stone and stucco, measuring 120 feet in diameter and rising to 54 feet at its peak, the Great Stupa is the oldest in the world. It was built by Emperor Asoka in the third century B.C.

Like most stupas, the Great Stupa is surrounded by a stone railing lining a processional path, where the faithful travel in ritual walks, always with the structure at their right. Inside the railing is a large terrace which served as an altar. The mound, or dome, rising from the terrace represents Mount Meru, home of the gods and the center of the universe.

At its crest is a three-tiered *chatravalis* (umbrella), a mark

of royalty. Four *toranas* (gateways) outside the stupa mark the points of the compass and represent the Four Noble Truths. These elaborately carved structures portray the Buddha as various symbols, including a lotus, which represents his birth; a tree, which represents his enlightenment; and a wheel, an emblem that he used in his first sermon. The *toranas* are considered the finest and earliest known specimens of Buddhist art.

Lying near the Great Stupa is a fragment of one of scores of polished sandstone pillars that King Asoka erected throughout his empire. Carved into these pillars are pledges to rule with kindness and truth, and warnings against disunity among Buddhists.

GREAT WALL OF CHINA

CHINA, C. 300 B.C.

The Great Wall spans 1,500 miles of mountains, deserts, and valleys in northern China. It is the largest building project in known history. Legends have surrounded the Great Wall ever since it was built in the third century B.C.

One tale claims that the twisting wall was once a huge dragon that stretched across China to protect the country from harm. Another says that Qin Shih-huang-ti, the first emperor of all China, who ordered the wall's construction, was a magician who rode a flying horse across the country, mapping the wall's route as he went.

The purpose of the Great Wall was twofold: it not only protected the new empire from raiders in the north, but it also served to mark the boundaries of the newly unified country. Varying in height from 15 to 50 feet and measuring 15 wide at the top, the wall was built on the foundations of earlier walls that had been erected along the borders of sepa-

rate Chinese states. Some historians believe that it was originally about 4,000 miles long.

The wall was completed in 20 years using more than 300,000 slaves, thousands of whom died under extremely harsh working conditions. To protect workers and supplies from attack, towers were constructed first and manned with soldiers. Each tower was "two arrow-shots" away from neighboring towers.

Today, only five of the thousands of original towers remain. Although Qin Shih-huang-ti's reign ended after 11 years, later emperors extended the Great Wall and strengthened its fortifications. During the Ming dynasty of A.D. 1368–1644, the aging Great Wall was extensively rebuilt.

PERSEPOLIS

IRAN, C. 520–330 B.C.

Once fabled for its wealth and splendor, Persepolis (Greek for "city of the Persians") is one of the greatest known architectural complexes of the ancient world. The city housed the king's residence and was the ceremonial hub of the Achaemenids, who swept through the Middle East in the sixth century B.C. and established the most powerful empire of the time.

Work on the palace complex spanned 60 years, beginning about 520 B.C. under King Darius I and continuing under Xerxes and Artaxerxes I. The remote location of Persepolis, 300 miles from the Persian capital of Susa, added an air of mystery to the king and his ceremonial rituals.

The architecture is a mix of Persian, Greek, Egyptian, and Assyrian elements, representative of the various cultures the Persians conquered. A monumental processional staircase on the west edge of the complex leads up to the Gate of Xerxes, guarded by immense sculptures of bulls. Scores of

elaborately carved columns, some measuring 65 feet, supported the roofs. Thirteen of these columns still stand.

The most important structures were the Throne Room, the 229-foot square Hall of 100 Columns, and the 195-foot square Apadana (audience hall). Palace rooms were extravagantly decorated with gold and colored tiles. The treasury housed the kings' riches, including precious metals, jewels, weapons, and valuable carpets.

In 330 B.C. the Greek warrior Alexander the Great captured Persepolis and ordered the splendid city burned to the ground. The ruins, now known as Takht-i-Jamshid, lay hidden until 1931, when they were excavated by archaeologists from the University of Chicago.

SUN TEMPLE

KONARAK, INDIA, 13TH CENTURY A.D.

Often called the Black Pagoda to distinguish it from the region's many white temples, the Sun Temple is the repository of many legends. One account says that after Samba, the son of Lord Krishna, contracted leprosy from his father's curse, he was cured by Surya, the Sun God. In Surya's honor, Samba built this massive temple. In actuality, the 13th-century king Narsimhadeva of the Ganga dynasty commissioned his chief architect, Sibai Santra, to erect this enormous tribute to Surya.

The temple was designed to resemble a colossal chariot. It appears to be mounted on 24 carved wheels, each 10 feet in diameter (representing the hours in one day), pulled by seven powerful horses (the days of the week). The three stepped tiers that form its pyramid-shaped dome hold colossal statues of important musicians and gods. Two smaller halls are separate from the main structure.

The walls of the Sun Temple are decorated with intricately carved scenes of every aspect of daily life, including a number of erotic images. Historians believe that the variety of the carvings was meant to suggest the sacredness of everyday life.

The building was never completed because of the Muslim conquest of India in the 13th century, and in an effort to prevent deterioration, the British lieutenant governor of Bengal in 1903 ordered the interior of the temple to be filled in. Nevertheless, the Sun Temple at Konarak remains a magnificent example of ancient Indian architecture.

TEMPLE OF HEAVEN

BEIJING, CHINA, A.D. 1420–1530

he Temple of Heaven, located just outside of the famous Forbidden City of ancient Chinese emperors, is one of the most remarkable architectural achievements in the world. The structure is actually three buildings erected in a straight line, with a 1,000-foot-long raised passage connecting the northern building, the Hall of Prayer for Good Harvests, with two southern buildings, the Imperial Vault of Heaven and the Circular Mound Altar. The complex is surrounded by an enclosure that is square at the south end (representing earth) and semicircular at the north end (representing heaven).

The Hall of Prayer for Good Harvests, shown here, is the largest and oldest building, erected in 1420 as a place of worship for emperors. The exquisitely carved temple is set on a circular, three-level terrace; it rises 125 feet high and is 100 feet in diameter. The deep blue glazed tile of its triple-tiered roof signifies the color of the heavens.

The structure is supported by 28 massive wooden columns: four central "dragon-well pillars" that represent the four seasons, and two sets of 12 pillars in concentric circles, representing the months of the year and the traditional divisions of day and night. It is said that this magnificent building was constructed entirely without nails.

The Imperial Vault of Heaven, erected in 1530, is a 64-foot-high circular temple with intricate arched roof supports. South of the Imperial Vault is the Circular Mound Altar, also built in 1530. It consists of three terraces of diminishing size, each ringed by nine stone circles. Both of these buildings, rebuilt in the 18th century, were meant to symbolize the geometric configuration of heaven.

EASTER ISLAND STATUES

RAPA NUI, CHILE, C. A.D. 1100–1680

N early 2,500 miles west of South America, the tiny island of Rapa Nui, more familiarly known as Easter Island, is home to a mysterious and fascinating group of ancient sculptures—huge statues with elongated human heads that stare inland. No one knows for sure where the island's first inhabitants came from or how they got there, but archaeologists have determined that people lived on the island by A.D. 400. The large statues for which Rapa Nui is famous were probably erected some time during A.D. 1100–1680.

The enormous statues sit on ceremonial platforms called *ahu*. They are made of white tuff, rock found in an extinct volcano on the eastern tip of the island. Each statue originally wore a topknot of red tuff and had eyes of white coral and red tuff. Most measure 10 to 20 feet high, although one statue is 32 feet high, and another, lying unfinished in an abandoned quarry, measures nearly 70 feet.

Using stone tools, sculptors carved the statues almost completely at the quarries, cutting out the front and sides of each head and working toward the back until only a narrow ridge connected the statue to the rock. Using a system of ropes, levers, and sleds, workers slowly moved the statues—each weighing about 50 tons—from the quarries and raised them into place.

What did the statues mean? A 17th-century visitor, Captain James Cook, claimed that natives told him they represented chiefs or regional kings. A more recent theory holds that they involved ancestor worship, a common practice on other South Pacific islands. Whatever their purpose, the immense statues remain a mute testimony to an ancient and enigmatic culture.

KUKULCÁN PYRAMID

N ow a popular tourist attraction, Chichén Itzá was once the cultural center of a Toltec-Mayan tribe, the Itzá. The city's name, which means "Mouth of the Wells of Itzá," reflects the tribe's dependence on an underground water supply that nourished the dry region in which the Itzá settled.

Chichén Itzá began as a small farming village around A.D. 500. Some time after 900, however, it became an important ceremonial center. Pilgrims from all over the region came to cast offerings into Chichén Itzá's *cenotes*, sacred wells dedicated to Tlaloc, the Toltec rain god. The Toltec believed that only great sacrifices would appease their fierce gods: archaeologists excavated 42 human skeletons from one well, along with gold medallions and pieces of jade.

The most impressive feature of Chichén Itzá, however, is the Kukulcán pyramid, dubbed "el Castillo" by 16th-century Spanish conquistadors because of its resemblance to a castle.

Built as a temple for the Toltec god Kukulcán, the keeper of the winds, it rises to 78 feet and covers an acre of ground. The nine terraces of the pyramid represent the levels of the Toltec underworld, and each of its four stairways has 365 steps, one for each day of the Toltec civil year. The temple walls are decorated with carved masks of gods and images of warriors engaged in battle.

Amazingly, since the Toltec did not have animals for transport, all the hewn stones for the temple were hauled by men. When archaeologists excavated the site of the Kukulcán pyramid, they discovered another, older structure beneath it, filled with treasures from an earlier period.

MACHU PICCHU

The mighty empire of the Incas stretched for more than 2,000 miles along the Pacific coast of South America and included parts of modern-day Ecuador, Peru, Bolivia, and Chile. In the 16th century the Spanish conquistador Francisco Pizarro captured and killed the emperor and plundered Incan cities, destroying the empire.

In 1911 a team of archaeologists made an amazing discovery. High on a mountaintop they came upon a magnificent fortress-like settlement. The town, Machu Picchu, named for the mountain on which it sits, was so isolated that the Spanish conquistadors had overlooked it in their campaign to destroy the Incan empire.

Machu Picchu's houses, temples, and other buildings were crafted from blocks of granite cut out of the mountain and fitted together without mortar. In the center of town is a large plaza, probably used for meetings, and a smaller plaza containing shrines and a temple. Most residences were one-story structures with open doorways covered by cloth and roofs made of thatched grass. The homes of important citizens surround the plazas. The poorer townspeople lived near the city wall in much smaller homes.

On the south slope of the mountain, the Inca created a system of terraces filled with gravel and topsoil from the river valley below. These gardens grew enough maize and vegetables to feed the town's population. Stonemasons cut basins and channels out of rock to collect and distribute water.

No one knows why the Incas chose this remote place to settle in. But the isolation of Machu Picchu allowed the town to remain undisturbed for hundreds of years, giving us a fascinating glimpse of an ancient and powerful civilization.

Pyramid of the Sun

Teotihuacán, Mexico, c. first century a.d.

Teotihuacán, located 33 miles northeast of Mexico City, was the largest and most important city in Mesoamerica (the southern region of North America before the arrival of European explorers). Beginning as a small settlement around 400 B.C., Teotihuacán grew into an urban center of great plazas, temples, palaces, and avenues. At the height of its influence, around A.D. 600, Teotihuacán was home to more than 150,000 people.

The city was the capital of the Olmec civilization, the earliest known culture to flourish in Mesoamerica and the most powerful, surpassing even the later Aztec empire. Teotihuacán was divided into quarters by two great avenues that crossed each other and formed the basis of a grid plan.

At the north end of the city sat the Pyramid of the Moon; to the south was the Temple of Quetzalcóatl (dedicated to the plumed serpent-god); and to the east was the

great Pyramid of the Sun, rising to 216 feet and measuring 720 by 760 feet at its base—a base area roughly equal to that of the massive pyramid of Cheops in Egypt.

The pyramid rises in four main stages, with a fifth, smaller stage between the third and fourth. On its west side, facing the Avenue of the Dead (the north-south artery), a grand stairway rises to the peak. Unlike the ancient Egyptians, the Olmec designed their pyramid to be climbed by priests and worshipers to be closer to their gods.

Some time during the seventh or eighth century, the Olmec civilization was sacked and burned by invaders called the Toltec. In the 14th century the Aztecs rediscovered the buried city and named it Teotihuacán—meaning "City of the Gods" or "Where Men Became Gods."

ACROPOLIS

ATHENS, GREECE, FIFTH CENTURY B.C.

On a small hill 300 feet above the modern city of Athens stands the holiest shrine of Athena, the goddess of wisdom and war. The Acropolis, or "high city," was the most sacred site of the ancient Greek empire. Between 460 and 400 B.C., during the period known as the Golden Age, the Greeks erected four major buildings as well as a number of smaller monuments and several statues, all honoring Athena, patroness of the city.

The principal entrance to the Acropolis runs through the Propylaea, an enormous marble gateway with five openings flanked by huge Doric columns. A ramp leading through the structure emerges in a similar gateway facing inward. The Propylaea has north and south wings, which are similar in design to the main building.

Southwest of the Propylaea stands a smaller structure dedicated to Athena as bringer of victory. Rebuilt twice in modern times from original ruins, it is decorated with friezes of mythological and historical battles. It is sometimes called the temple of Nike Apteros ("wingless victory").

The main temple of Athena is the Parthenon, the largest building on the Acropolis. An architectural masterpiece, it remains the most important monument of ancient Greek civilization. Built between 447 and 432 B.C. of brilliant white marble, it stands on a platform surrounded by 46 Doric columns. Colonnades divided the interior into a broad nave and side aisles decorated with relief sculpture, much of which still exists. At its west end once stood a huge gold and ivory statue of Athena. North of the Parthenon is the Erechtheion, a complex structure dedicated to Athena, Erechtheum (an early Greek king), and Poseidon (god of the sea).

AVENUE OF LIONS

DELOS, GREECE, C. SEVENTH CENTURY B.C.

The tiny Greek island of Delos, slightly more than a square mile in area, is one of about 220 islands in the Aegean Sea known collectively as the Cyclades. Yet during ancient times Delos was the most important of these islands. There, according to Greek legend, the goddess Leto gave birth to Apollo, the sun god, and his twin, Artemis, the huntress goddess of the moon.

During the eighth and seventh centuries B.C., Delos was the religious and political center of the Ionian States, which later evolved into the Greek empire centered in Athens. In the third century B.C. Delos became independent and was the commercial center of the Aegean Sea. By the second century A.D., however, the once sacred island was largely deserted.

Beginning in the 1870s, archaeological excavations unearthed a sanctuary complex that gives us a glimpse of ancient Ionian religious life. Among its structures are the

temples of Apollo and Artemis, as well as a number of smaller temples and monuments.

Lining the sanctuary of Delos to the north is a series of marble statues known as the Avenue of the Lions or the Lion Terrace. These figures, which date to the seventh century B.C., functioned as the eternal guardians of the sacred lake where Apollo and Artemis were said to have been born. Only five lions remain intact (a sixth was moved to Venice, Italy, in the 17th century), but historians believe that they originally numbered 14 or 16. Although the Lion Terrace was dedicated to Apollo, the figures actually seem to be lionesses and may have been erected to honor female gods worshiped on the island.

COLOSSEUM

ROME, ITALY, A.D. 69–80

The Colosseum, the greatest ancient wonder in Italy, was formally known as the Flavian Amphitheater. It takes its popular name from a 120-foot-high statue, or "colossus," of the Emperor Nero. The amphitheater was the scene of bloodthirsty contests among men and savage animals—a popular form of Roman entertainment called "the games."

The Roman emperor Vespasian began construction of the amphitheater; it was completed by his son Titus about 12 years later. Despite damage from several earthquakes and the removal of masonry during the Middle Ages for use in other buildings, much of the Colosseum is still standing.

The oval-shaped building stood 160 feet high and measured 618 feet long by 510 feet wide. The exterior was made of carved travertine marble; the interior of a porous rock called tufa. The ramp for the seating area, which held 50,000 to 55,000 spectators, was made of concrete slabs.

The arches of the outer wall were framed by three styles of columns: Doric on the ground floor, Ionic on the second level, and Corinthian, the most elaborate, on the third level. Eighty entrances, through arches on the ground floor, allowed for easy access.

A heavy wooden floor concealed a complex of underground chambers which housed ravenous and often exotic animals such as lions, tigers, leopards, rhinoceroses, and bears. The chambers also held prisoners and slaves, called gladiators, trained to fight for entertainment. The most popular events were gladiator fights and staged wild animal hunts, although Roman crowds also enjoyed watching wild beasts attack and kill humans. These "sports" were forbidden by law in later centuries.

DELPHI

GREECE, 650 B.C. TO A.D. 150

In Greek mythology, the god Zeus, seeking the center of the world, released two eagles at the same moment from the western and eastern ends of the earth. The eagles met at Delphi, on the lower slopes of Mount Parnassus. There, at the exact point where the eagles met, an oval stone called the *omphalos* was placed in the fourth century B.C. to remind visitors that Delphi was the "navel" of the world.

The most sacred site at Delphi was the temple dedicated to Apollo, the god of light, poetry, and music. The Greeks believed that Apollo could also foresee the future. To learn their fate, they began consulting an oracle (a person through whom a god is presumed to speak).

This ritual became so widespread that monarchs and heroes from as far away as Asia Minor, North Africa, and Sicily traveled to Delphi, bringing lavish gifts that enriched the town and enhanced its reputation as the center of the

world. The practice continued even after the Greeks were overthrown by the Romans, but the spread of Christianity diminished the powerful influence of the oracle at Delphi.

Excavations of Delphi began in 1893. In an area called the Sanctuary, archaeologists discovered ruins of the Temples of Apollo and Athena, a theater, and treasury buildings holding thousands of statues, architectural pieces, and works of art from the major cities of ancient Greece. Outside the Sanctuary walls, they uncovered buildings such as the Stadium, where athletic events took place, and the Gymnasium, where the city's youths practiced athletics and attended school. Also unearthed was the magnificent Tholos (shown here), a beautifully crafted, multicolored circular building; its function remains unknown.

HADRIAN'S WALL

NORTHUMBRIA, ENGLAND, A.D. 122–132

amed after the ruler who ordered its construction in A.D. 122, Hadrian's Wall marked the northernmost edge of the Roman Empire. At the height of its power, the Empire controlled most of Europe, North Africa, and the Middle East.

It had a huge army, whose soldiers were also trained to build roads, complete with bridges and viaducts (a series of arches) over rivers or steep valleys. The roads enabled troops to move more quickly and efficiently and improved trade throughout the region.

To complete the wall, Hadrian employed a crew of professional soldiers and legionaries who labored for more than 10 years. The structure, made mostly of stone, measured 73 miles long and reached to 15 feet high and 8 feet deep in places. It spanned the width of Great Britain. Both north and south faces were protected by deep ditches.

At each Roman mile (slightly less than the modern mile)

stood a "milecastle," a fort manned by at least eight soldiers. Turrets between the milecastles allowed sentries to observe all traffic across the wall. Over time, civilian villages formed around the forts built along the south side of the wall to house soldiers and supplies.

Hadrian's Wall had several purposes: to mark the frontier of the Roman Empire, to serve as a toll-gathering system, and to defend the empire from northern attacks. As the Empire declined during the early fifth century, it began neglecting frontier settlements. The wall fell into disrepair as local inhabitants carried off stones for their homes, fields, and churches. Today only fragments of the original structure remain.

SKARA BRAE

ORKNEY ISLANDS, SCOTLAND, C. 3100–2500 B.C.

The village of Skara Brae was discovered in 1850 when a violent storm blew away the sands covering its walls. It is one of the most remarkable prehistoric sites in Europe: a collection of rectangular huts with stone walls up to six feet thick, protected from high winds, cold, and enemies by mounds of earth and debris called middens.

The walls of each hut are corbeled, or stepped, so that the roof is narrower than the floor. The huts were connected by covered passageways so that inhabitants could move from one room to another without leaving the complex.

Inside each dwelling is a central hearth, a raised area containing bones and cooking pots, stone shelf units, and stone box beds. Archaeologists also discovered stone boxes sunk into the dirt floors, which probably served as tanks for live fishing bait. Off the main rooms, smaller areas served by a drainage system are believed to have been privies.

An excavation during the 1920s dated Skara Brae at circa 500 B.C., but later investigations dated bones found there at about 5,000 years old. The settlement appears to have been a self-contained community where household items, tools, clothing, and decorative objects were created. Intricately carved stone objects show that the inhabitants were skilled stonemasons. Markings on some of the stones found at Skara Brae also suggest that a primitive writing system had developed.

No one knows for certain why or how Skara Brae was abandoned. Layers of rubbish found inside the huts were carefully placed, leading archaeologists to conclude that the practice was part of a religious ceremony meant to prevent the homes from being reoccupied. But the fate of the original villagers remains a mystery.

STONEHENGE

tonehenge is one of the most famous and mysterious prehistoric sites in the world. Man-made structures of one kind or another have existed at Stonehenge for thousands of years, yet no one is exactly sure who built them or what their purpose was.

Archaeologists believe that the first configuration on the site—a round, wooden building surrounded by a circular ditch and a bank 20 feet wide and six feet high—was constructed between 3200 and 2700 B.C. The building, now gone, probably served as a mortuary, where the dead were stored before cremation or burial. Some time between 2700 and 2200 B.C., 56 pits (called "Aubrey holes" after John Aubrey, the 18th-century scientist who discovered them) were dug in a circle inside the original bank. Historians speculate that the region's inhabitants poured libations (liquid offerings) into the holes to appease their gods.

Between 2200 and 2000 B.C., builders began erecting circles made of a type of stone found about 200 miles away. Between 2000 and 1600 B.C. the huge slabs shown in the photograph were erected. The task of moving the limestone to the site was remarkable enough, but the exactitude with which they were positioned is astounding: despite the sloping ground, the lintels placed horizontally atop the 13-foot slabs are exactly level.

Far outside the original circular ditch sits another slab called the Heel Stone. Each year on the morning of the summer solstice, the sun rises directly above the Heel Stone, and a shaft of sunlight casts deep shadows across the limestone uprights. Because of this phenomenon and other alignments detected among the formations of Stonehenge, some believe it was once a celestial observatory.

TEMPLE OF DEMETER

PAESTUM, ITALY, C. 540–510 B.C.

irst known as Posidonia, the ancient city of Paestum was founded by Greeks around 600 B.C. The city is famous today for the three Doric structures that have survived: the Temple of Hera I (the Basilica), the Temple of Hera II (also called the Temple of Poseidon), and the Temple of Demeter (also known as the Temple of Ceres). In Greek mythology, Hera was the queen of Olympian gods, the wife and sister of Zeus, and the protectress of women, marriage, and childbirth. Demeter, Hera's sister, was the goddess of harvest and fertility.

The Temple of Demeter was the second of the three built at Posidonia, and much of it has survived, including all of its fluted columns and portions of the west and east pediments (the triangular sections resting atop the columns at either end of the temple). The area directly below the pediments was probably decorated with reliefs and statues, which

would have been painted in bright colors, especially traditional red and blue.

The main room would have housed a statue of Demeter, and a storeroom held the treasures collected in her honor. Like the temples of Hera I and Hera II, the Temple of Demeter faces east, so that the ancient Greeks, who held their worship ceremonies outside of the buildings, looked toward the rising sun.

Toward the end of the fifth century B.C., the city fell into the hands of the Romans and was later renamed Paestum. In modern times, archaeologists discovered an underground building near the Temple of Demeter that held several iron spits (or bars) and eight bronze vessels from the sixth century B.C. that still contained honey.

CHRONOLOGY

c. 3200 B.C.	Earliest configuration at Stonehenge.
c. 3100–2500 B.C.	Skara Brae village, Orkney Islands, Scotland.
c. 2550–2490 B.C.	Giza pyramids and Great Sphinx built.
c. 1800–900 B.C.	First village settlements in Peru.
c. 1411–1375 B.C.	Temple of Luxor, Egypt, constructed.
Eighth century B.C.	Delos, Greece, becomes religious and political center of the Ionian states.
c. 776 B.C.	First Olympic Games held in Greece.
650 B.C.	Delphi, Greece, rises to prominence.
c. 540–510 B.C.	Posidonia, later known as Paestum, Italy, founded by the Greeks.
520 B.C.	City of Persepolis established.
Fifth century B.C.	Acropolis constructed in Greece.
c. 300 B.C.	Great Wall of China erected.
c. 250 B.C.	Great Stupa at Sanchi, India, built.
c. First century A.D.	Teotihuacán, Mexico, founded.
43	Romans invade and conquer Britain.
69–80	Colosseum of Rome built.
122–132	Hadrian's Wall erected.
320	Gupta dynasty founded in India.

600	Teotihuacán, Mexico, becomes capital of the Olmec tribe.
950	Chichén Itzá, Mexico, emerges as cultural center of Toltec-Maya tribe.
1090	Ananda Temple built in Pagan, Burma (now Myanmar).
1100–1680	Easter Island statues erected.
1113–1150	Angkor Wat built.
13th century	Sun Temple constructed in Konarak, India.
1252	Great Buddha of Kamakura, Japan, erected.
1420–1530	Temple of Heaven constructed in Peking (now Beijing), China.
1438	Inca empire of Peru at its height.
c. 1440–1570	Machu Picchu established by the Incas.

INDEX ✦

FURTHER READING

Book Division, National Geographic Society. *Mysteries of Mankind: Earth's Unexplained Landmarks.* Washington, DC: National Geographic Society, 1992.

Cotterell, Arthur. *Ancient China.* New York: DK Publishing, 1994.

Ingpen, Robert, and Wilkinson, Philip. *Encyclopedia of Mysterious Places.* Surrey, England: Dragon's World, 1991.

McKeever, Susan. *Ancient Rome.* New York: DK Publishing, 1995.

Millard, Anne. *The Atlas of Ancient Worlds.* New York: DK Publishing, 1994.

Putnam, James, and Hart, George. *Ancient Egyptians.* New York: DK Publishing, 1996.

Wilkinson, Philip, and Pollard, Michael. *The Magical East.* Philadelphia: Chelsea House, 1994.

Wilkinson, Philip, and Pollard, Michael. *The Master Builders.* Philadelphia: Chelsea House, 1994.